The Phenomenal Human

ALSO BY NGOZI OLIVIA OSUOHA

The Transformation Train
Letter to My Unborn
Sensation
Tropical Escape (with Amos O. Ojwang')
Fruits from the Poetry Planet
Poetic Grenade
Whispers of the Biafran Skeleton
Chains
Raindrops
Freeborn
Eclipse of Tides
The Subterfuge
Green Snake on a Green Grass
Chariots of Archangels
Wonderment
Interwoven
xenophobicracy
Destiny

The Phenomenal Human

**poems by
Ngozi Olivia Osuoha**

Poetic Justice Books
Port St. Lucie, Florida

©2020 Ngozi Olivia Osuoha

book design and layout: SpiNDec, Port Saint Lucie, FL
cover image: Woyo Mask, DRC | LACMA
cover design: Kris Haggblom

All rights reserved.

No part of this book may be used or reproduced in any manner whatsoever without written permission except in the case of brief quotations embodied in critical articles and reviews. Members of educational institutions and organizations wishing to photocopy any of the work for classroom use, or authors, artists and publishers who would like to obtain permission for any material in the work, should contact the publisher.

Printed in the United States of America.
Published by Poetic Justice Books
Port Saint Lucie, Florida
www.poeticjusticebooks.com

ISBN: 978-1-950433-42-1

FIRST EDITION
10 9 8 7 6 5 4 3 2 1

to Humanity and those who serve Humanity

contents

TIME	3
LIFE	4
BIRTH	5
DEATH	6
GROWTH	7
GENERATION	8
RAIN	9
SUN	10
MOON	11
STARS	12
LIGHT	13
DARKNESS	14
EARTH	15
GOD	16
SPIRIT	17
SOUL	18
RELIGION	19
CRY	20
LAUGHTER	21
MOOD	22
RAINBOW	23
MIST	24
DEW	25
SENSATION	26
SEASON	27
REASON	28
SEX	29
WATER	30
FOOD	31
OCEAN	32

RIVER	33
STREAM	34
ANGER	35
HAPPINESS	36
TALENT	37
TIDE	38
WAVE	39
STORM	40
HATE	41
DREAM	42
SLEEP	43
THIRST	44
HUNGER	45
LOVE	46
WILL	47
PASSION	48
DANCE	49
HUMANITY	50
AGE	51
PUZZLE	52
QUESTION	53
FUTURE	54
HISTORY	55
LEGACY	56
THEORY	57
ADVENTURE	58
INNOVATION	59
JUSTICE	60

UNITY	61
PEACE	62
EQUITY	63
SIGN	64
MISSION	65
ECLIPSE	66
POPULATION	67
CLIMATE	68
TEMPERATURE	69
NATURAL DISASTERS	70
ACT OF GOD	71
RACISM	72
GERMINATION	73
BREATH	74
THUNDER	75
RELATIONSHIPS	76
NATURAL RESOURCES	77
VEGETATION	78
MARRIAGE	79
DIVORCE	80
MOUNTAIN	82
LEARNING	84
GALAXY	86
VOICE	87
BLOOD	88
ORIGIN	89
RACE	90
PARENT	91

CHANGE	92
FIGHT	93
SIBLINGS	94
FOUNDER	95
CREATIVITY	96
FRUITS	97
SKILL	98
FLEXIBILITY	99
AGILITY	100
REPRODUCTION	101
LUST	102
URGE	103
THE PHENOMENAL HUMAN	105

The Phenomenal Human

TIME

Time is a constant
Ticking all the time,
Through time.

Time is a slippery phenomenon
Always on the move
Reaching destinations,
Through men.

Time is a reminder
Accurate recorder
It calculates, it gathers
Reconciling life with death,
And death to life.

Time, time, time
You can be like time
You can be a time,
Keep time, mark time
If you want to be forever.

The one who equates time
Living from the past
Living for the present
Living for the future,
Counting all, analyzing them,
That one is the phenomenal human.

Time fades, fading or not
Time stands tests and tastes,
Time never dies,
Time is phenomenal
Be time, be timely, you human.

Ngozi Olivia Osuoha

LIFE

Life is life
It is the essence of living
Life is a phenomenon.

Either you live
You are alive,
Or you die
You are dead,
Live life to the fullest
So that dying will be worth it.

Be a life, be alive
Live, be a living soul
Stay alive, be phenomenal
Be a phenomenon too.

Life is the only existence
Nothing more, nothing less
The reason of being in the world
Is to live, amidst troubles
Live phenomenally.

Living is full of work
Dying is the tail end
Whether fairy tales or cocktails.

Phenomenal humans live forever
By being life, alive, and a life
Breathe into others
Give them life to live.

BIRTH

Birth is constant
It is as constant as change
It is in fact, change.

Birth is the prove of multiplication
And the seal of reproduction,
Birth is an assignment
A phenomenal duty of man.

Birth announces life
And increases hope,
Birth is a phenomenon
Be one, be a phenomenal human.

Birth records growth
And applauds addition
Birth is a surplus
Born, be birth, be born.

Birth ideas, birth visions
Birth change, great change
Positive and creative
Phenomenal birth, greatness
Unique births and rebirths.

Birth is nature
Nature makes it rich,
Birth is divine, celestial
Phenomenal humans birth reality.

DEATH

Death is nature
It is an inevitable end
Especially to living things,
Even non living things die too
When their usefulness and lifespan elapse.

Death is a phenomenon
It is not stoppable
Man live with it
Waiting to die someday.

Death is a track
A runway for everyone
Leading to somewhere,
A strange place
Where reversion is impossible.

Good or bad, rich or poor
Death awaits all,
Tall or short, big or small
Educated, illiterate, famous or unknown
Death waits.

Death is of many types
Physical, spiritual, mental, social
Religious, political, educational, and others
However, physical we know well
And that hurts us more.

If you want to be phenomenal
Be inevitable, be huge
Be a striking force,
Though not like death.

GROWTH

Growth is a phenomenon
Hidden from the eyes
But experienced and felt
Many processes and patterns
Several procedures and tactics
Natural, complex yet simple.

Growth is beyond humans
It is a wonder and a puzzle
Yet we see the physical part
And the ones we may see,
Especially in physical ways.

Spiritual growth, mental growth
Financial, social, marital growths
There are many kinds.

Be growth, grow, change
Let the world feel you
Let the world acknowledge you
Be a phenomenon, a phenomenal growth
Because life is about growth.

GENERATION

Generation is a phenomenon
It comes and goes
Thousands of people,
Men and women.

Generation begets generation
They bear signs and wonders,
They transfer cultures
Ethics, norms, and values.

Be a generation, great
Be a force, factorial, frictional, gravitational
Be a voice, be heard
Be a phenomenon.

A generation is thirty years
People live more than that
Some never live up to that,
But it matters we be felt.
Live like a generation.
Impact generations
Be phenomenal,
Especially in a phenomenal world.

RAIN

Rain is natural
It comes from above
It waters the earth
To satisfy man
And enrich the land,
Rain is a phenomenon.

Rain is unusual
Yet, very usual
It does not originate from here
It goes through some processes
Rain, is phenomenal.

Be a rain, rain on earth
Bless the world
Saturate the earth
Water men and women
Let them be blessed.

Reign, rain, you are a phenomenon
Be a phenomenal rain
Rain until the earth is full
Drizzle, rain, heavy and light
Bless the earth, you phenomenon.

Ngozi Olivia Osuoha

SUN

Sun is a fact
A fact we see always
We know little or nothing
It bewilders creations.
Sun is a natural phenomenon
Up there it sits
Still it rises, it sets
It affects the earth
And keeps it warm or hot.

Be warm, warm the earth
Be hot, hot the world
Be dry, dry the earth,
Be that, phenomenal.

The sun is great
It says a whole lot
The sun heals the world
And teaches her, mysteries.

Be a phenomenon, be the sun
The phenomenal sun,
Be sunlight, be nature
The sun can lead you home.

MOON

The moon is a light
It shines at night
It chases darkness
And lights up the world.

The moon is a phenomenon
It cannot be killed
It is programmed like destiny
It gives excellent time
And tales are told under it.

The moon is a god
Some people worship it
A lot happens at full moon
The moon is very powerful.

Be a moon, be the moon
Chase away darkness in the world
Enlighten people everywhere
Be a phenomenon.

Night is dark, dark is the night
Be full, like the moon
At worst, be half moon
Let the world see light at night,
Yes, especially your light.

Ngozi Olivia Osuoha

STARS

Twinkle, twinkle, dear star
Light up the world at night,
Let those in darkness merry
For their light has come.

Twinkle, shine, glow, O star
Far, far, beyond comprehension
Be a wonder that you are.

Shine, sparkle, dazzle, well
Crystal clear, be seen around
Loud, clear, be heard all over
Feel the world with awe.

Shine, phenomenal human
Glow, you are a fact
Dazzle, confuse darkness
Let the world admire you.

Stars are phenomenal
The star is a phenomenon
Be a star, be phenomenal
Let the many, stick your shine.

LIGHT

Light, light is a gift
Daylight, or artificial light
Nature bids light well.

Light shines in darkness
And darkness disappears
Light wins all the time
You too, can shine that way.

Light is a wonder
Even when overlooked
Light is a phenomenon
It tells the power of God.

Be a light in the day
Be a light in the dark,
Be a light in the world
Let the universe behold your light
Let darkness celebrate your light,
You are a phenomenon,
Shine phenomenally.

Light is light, light is great
Be bright, be light
Capture the phenomenal light.

DARKNESS

Darkness is natural
It comes and goes,
Yes, mostly at night
It scares, it comes deep
Leaving wonders for the morning.

Darkness is of some types
In life, in career, in age, in choice
In dream, in work, in marriage
It varies, it is many
But darkness of time is really dark.

The night, short or long
The wait, fearful, dreadful and deadly
Longing, praying, hoping
But the day, short or long
The sight is clear and pure.

Darkness is natural
But none likes it
Light is more preferable
In all areas of life and light
Chase off darkness
By being the phenomenal light.

EARTH

The earth is amazing
More amazing than others
We live here all long
We die here, too.

Generations upon generations
Men and women, great and small
Discoveries, times and ages
Tongues and tribes, diversity.

The earth is a phenomenon
Housing all kinds of phenomena
Spherical in shape
Revolving, according to geography
Large and millions in width
Accommodating wonders, vast
Phenomenon, phenomenal.

Be the earth
Yes, you can
Revolve, rotate, house, accommodate
Grow, cherish, welcome
Learn, relearn, unlearn, embrace
Be a phenomenon, be a wonder
For mother earth is a puzzle.

GOD

God is mystery
None can fathom Him
He made the world
And all in it,
He is invisible
And invincible,
Nothing can destroy Him.

He made us in His image
Gave us diverse powers
And many gifts,
He made us little gods
A little lower than the angels.

Little gods are phenomenal
Push up over the limits
Whatever limits are there,
Embrace it realistically and phenomenally
Let it be seen.

Be courageous, be brave
You are celestial, you are unique
Work, walk, like a god.

SPIRIT

Spirits are unseen
They are numerous, uncountable
Good and bad ones
Some save, some hurt
Some deliver,some foment.

They are not seen
Except in rare occasions
For some who testify so,
We too, are spirits
If we see ourselves that way.

We have spirit,
Heart, body and soul
We function with them all
So we can fly as phenomenal humans.

Be a spirit, a good one
Save, deliver, live beyond
Be phenomenal, yes
The phenomenal human does wonders
Because he is greatly extraordinary.

SOUL

We are souls
Souls living in flesh
We are souls
Souls with blood,
We are a world
Physical world, here.

Our souls depart at death
They leave our body
Flesh and blood, away.

Be a soul, yes that soul
That phenomenal soul that inspires,
Inspire the world
Salvage the earth,
Rescue the land
Let your soul live on.

Phenomenal soul, ancient
Soaring like the eagle
Seeing far beyond
Yes, that phenomenal soul.

RELIGION

Religion, the most phenomenal
The one that also harms
Different beliefs for different religions.

Religion produces phenomena
Fooling many and deceiving most
Washing out facts and creating scenes
Phenomenal religion, horrors too.

Men of terrible characters
Humans of ulterior motives
Beings of raw evil
Adulterating God and divinity.

Phenomenal madness, mentality
Cooking and serving craziness,
Tracking down giants,
Falling the elect
And capturing the sacred.

Be not a phenomenal fool
Or a deceit of phenomena,
Help cleanse religion
It is full of errors, manmade
Only then you can be a phenomenal human.

Ngozi Olivia Osuoha

CRY

Cry is real and natural
But not all cries are good,
Many are for mourning
Loss, and mostly negative.

However, there are good tears
Tears of joy
Tears of reconciliation
Tears of victory
So much types of tears.

The ones shed when our joy is full
The ones full of testimonies
Positive and green stories.

Therefore make people shed these tears
Let them shed phenomenal tears
Unforgettable and memorable tears.

Cause people to wear smiles
Smiles of pure laughter,
Give them peace and happiness
Spread love and unity
Be a phenomenal cause of tears of joy.

LAUGHTER

Laughter is great
It is even medicinal
Laughter is a healing and a healing tool
It is also a therapy,
Laughter brightens the day
And relaxes the body,
It helps a lot to laugh
Even in the face of pain
No matter how difficult it is.

Laughter is a phenomenon
Laugh, as often as possible
Make people laugh too
Do not mock people
Because life is not fair,
Rather help them find laughter.

Be the phenomenal laughter
The one that erases pain
That laughter that dries off tears
Laugh, laugh, let them laugh
Teach them how to laugh
Laugh away your sorrow
Make that phenomenal laughter happen.

Not just opening your mouth
And flashing your dentition,
Spur yourself to laugh
Laughter does not cost much
Stand up, work, fight
Win, only then you can laugh loud and louder
Even losing will not cause more pain.

Ngozi Olivia Osuoha

MOOD

Mood is normal too
It is of many types
It varies with people
Depending on times and issues.

Circumstances are many, too
And they all bring moods
Different people, different approaches
Moods swing with time.

Place, event, reason, people
All come with moods,
However, the best is happiness.

Be the reason for happiness
Phenomenal happiness to people
Make others happy
Let it be planted
And recorded in your name.

Mood is a phenomenon
No matter who is involved,
Be then, the phenomenal human.

RAINBOW

O beautiful rainbow
Heavenly body at its best
Beauty beyond measure
Where colours sing and praise
Rainbow, where colours merge.

O the beautiful rainbow
The most beautiful of creation
Significant, symbolic, unique
Super, great, elegant
You speak volume, yet unheard
Phenomenal, important.

Be the rainbow in our cloud
Be a rainbow in our sky
Be beautiful, merge with others
Say excellent things
Do phenomenal things, be rainbow.

Spread colours of love
Paint colours of peace
Share true colours of unity,
Be the phenomenal rainbow.

Ngozi Olivia Osuoha

MIST

The mist, wet and cold
Cooling the morning
Blessing the new day
Speaking to the earth
Encouraging vegetation.

O shower, like blessing
Drizzle, faint or bold
Bless, bless, keep blessing
Let the phenomenon be known.

You can be the mist
Early morning blessings
You can drizzle upon the earth
Share your positive vibes
Let the dry world be in tune
Wet the land, let it grow.

The earth needs you
The world needs you
Yes, you, this you
Because you are amazing
You are a phenomenal human.

DEW

Dew of blessed nature
Drizzling like peace
Announcing a rebirth,
Rebirth of happiness.

Dews; early, peaceful
Chilling, cooling, romancing
Dews; cool, cooling, calm.

Dews: morning dews of newness
Singing songs of exaltation
Honouring freedom and victory
Dews; trumpeting readiness
Harping melodies of love,
Be dews, dews of phenomenal heavens.

Phenomenal dews upon the earth
Showering blessings and humours
Guarding tribes and tongues
Cheering strength and power
Lifting valour and courage
Refreshing bravery and passion.

Be dews, be dews, phenomenal dews
Sit on pews, settle on pews
Let sitters be refreshed,
Yes, you, I mean you
You can, absolutely.

Ngozi Olivia Osuoha

SENSATION

Sensation of deep message
Sending waves down the spine
Charging souls to be up
Warming up bodies,
Caressing the future.

Yes, sensation; phenomenal
Sensational phenomenon
Thoughts of life, sensational
Living among angels
Calling forth the dead
To arise and shine.

Phenomenal sensation, you, yes
You are, yes of course
Sensitize the world, the whole
In a bit, bit by bit
In a bid to rule, rule the world.

Sensational humans, they do
They change the world
Whether they live long or short
You are a sensation,
Return it, lie it, harness it
Be a phenomenal sensation
Let the world feel it.

SEASON

There are many seasons
Times are numerous
Times fit into us
We fit into times, as well.

Seasons differ, too
They serve their purposes in our life
We live with them for them
We flow and take their shape,
As if they are water
And we, containers.

Seasons come to bless us
They are so endowed with nature
Seasons are great, and mysterious too.

Fair seasons, unfair ones
The ones that usher in freedom
The ones that bring hardship
Depending on fate and destiny.

But we are seasons too
We happen, and things happen
We happen at life
And life happens to us,
Whichever way, we are there.

We are created to recreate and procreate
So we are seasonal as well,
In and out of season
Phenomenal humans, in phenomenal seasons.

Ngozi Olivia Osuoha

REASON

Reasons abound for actions
Reasons speak for reactions too,
Every reason pumps up something,
In defense, support, for or against.

Reasons can be real and funny
They can be horrible or queer
Reasons fail us sometimes.

Some reasons are phenomenal
And phenomenal humans utilize them.

Be the reason for some joy
And others' happiness
Set the track straight
And the record great,
Whether small or big
Make phenomenal things
Yes, you can, we can.

Be a phenomenal human
Let the phenomena live on,
The world is in need of it.

SEX

Sex is life
A part of nature
It gives pleasure
And it helps procreation.

Sex is of male and female
Each complimenting each other
Emotionally, and otherwise.

Sex is a wonder
Raw, real and natural
It serves many purposes
Pleasure, satisfaction, and more.

Without sex, the world will be lost
Empty and scanty,
Lonely, boring and timid.

Be like sex, male or female
Put people high, positive change
Not rape, not lust
Bring them together, intimate
Be phenomenal, be true.

WATER

Water is great
It gives energy
And satisfies life,
Water quenches thirst
And enables growth
All living things need water.

Water has no enemy
It does not segregate
No racism, no tribalism
Water is not a sadist
Nor is it a terrorist,
Be like water
Save life, improve health
Facilitate growth, satisfy urge
Help vegetation and mankind.

Save humanity like water
Water cleans and purifies
Water flushes dirts
Water is amazing
Phenomenal water.

Quench people's yearnings
Help them find rest
Be like water, be phenomenal.

FOOD

Food is a necessity
It is vital to the human survival
Food builds the body
And sustains growth,
Food replenishes dead tissues
And revives the body system,
Food grows the cells
And maintains organs
Food fights bacteria
And supports health,
Food is wonderful
An incredible phenomenon,
It prolongs life
And oils lifespan.

Be food, be vital, be lively
Grow men and women
Grow the human system and society,
Feed mankind in words and deeds
Be phenomenal, be a phenomenon.

Yes, you, you can, we can
We can feed the world
By being phenomenal food,
Let people feed on you
Let the world be fed by you
Through you, in you, because of you
Because we are phenomenal humans.

OCEAN

Ocean, a gorgeous creature
Natural and mysterious,
Full of acquatic life,
Far beyond imagination.

Ocean, in different lands
Pride of continents
Glory of worlds apart
Hope of nations unborn.

Ocean, great and mighty
Means of discovery and movements,
Tales of adventure and research.

Ocean, unique, spectacular
You are an ocean
Ocean, phenomenal
Phenomenal ocean,
Yes, you are one, remain so.

Be an ocean, a phenomenal ocean
Lead nations, move them
Transport cargoes, connect people
Let your life be like an ocean.

Sustain lives, numerous
Harbour homes, diverse
Let worlds anchor on you,
You are nothing but a phenomenal human.

RIVER

River of life
Flowing through life
Giving breath to aquatics.

River of life, beautiful
Overflowing within banks
Clean, sparkling, wonderful.

River of life
Life of a river
Living, flowing, rich
Never drying, always neat.

Phenomenal river
Flowing for man
Teaching phenomena
Exploring bounds and limits.

The phenomenal human
Flowing like a river
Never giving up
Keep flowing all round
North, south, east and west.

Ngozi Olivia Osuoha

STREAM

Stream, beautiful stream
Rural stream for thirst
Like a spring, clean
Ready, for the people.

Spring, spring of life
Stream, pure, natural
Far or near, for the people
Healing, cleaning the land.

Stream of fairy tales
Ancient miracles of old
Tales of unbelievable wonder
Amazing gift of nature.

Healing, purifying, sanctifying
Blessing, fortifying, consecrating
Retain that power of old
Let the lost be found.

Phenomenal stream and spring
One in all, all in one
Touch the weak, and the feeble
Take away poverty.

Yes, the phenomenal human
The light and love of the world
Sprinkle your drops and dews
Let the thirst quench.

ANGER

Anger is natural
From the beginning of the world
It is a part of man.

Anger is inborn, inbuilt
No one can take it away
Anger is of different types
Some are dangerous
Some are righteous.

Dangerous anger do horrors
Righteous anger do wonders,
Choose one, choose wisely
Be phenomenal,
Dangerous anger can be managed
Manage it well, appropriately
Work on it, subdue it.

Anger of phenomenon
Phenomenal anger pays
The one that produces good
That which reconciles, revives
Be angry for phenomenal purposes.

Control your negativity
Cage it, rule it, lead it
Be the phenomenal human.

Ngozi Olivia Osuoha

HAPPINESS

Happiness is a force
It radiates from inside
Different things make us happy.

Happiness is a relief
It cures, it heals
It liberates the soul
And uplifts the spirit.

Happiness is wonderful
It can bring back the lost
Happiness moves mountains
It can seal peace,
And water unions
Happiness helps love
It evacuates sorrow
And plants unity.

Be happy always
Make others happy too
Be a happy force
Be a phenomenal happiness
And a phenomenon for happiness,
Share it wherever you go.

TALENT

Talent is raw
It is hidden in men
Talent is pure
It is divinely placed
Talent is sacred
Only the Creator gives it
He gives freely as He wishes
According to power and might
Depending on mission and purpose.

Discover your talent
Use it phenomenally
Harness others' talents
Channel them to the glory of God.

Talent does not die
Except we kill it,
Talent does not fade
Except we allow it age.

Use yours, use it well
Help others, teach them
Make this phenomenon so phenomenal.

Ngozi Olivia Osuoha

TIDE

Tide of the sea
Tide of the ocean
Strong like nature
Real like reality,
Great and amazing
Tide, rolling up and down.

Tide, the force of sea
Tide, the current of ocean
Powerful movement
Waiting for no one.

A great phenomenon
Creating ripples, mighty
Sweeping off anything.

Be a tide, be mighty
Sweep off dirts around
Let your current overflow
Travel far and wide.

Be this phenomenon today
Tomorrow, and phenomenal,
Move the sea and ocean.

WAVE

Wave, great wave
Looking at no man
Rowing its way,
Travelling through time,
Clearing its path
Gigantic, fierce and great.

Wave, waving man
Flying like kites
Ceaseless, fearless, tireless
Moving in one accord
Facing whatever comes
Wave, waving god.

Be a wave, loud and aloud
High, long, real and hot
Warding off obstacles
Casting out demons,
Because you are phenomenal.

Phenomenal wave of human
Changing the world for good
Cleansing the land of evil,
Go on, keep doing it
Fear not, be strong
You are forceful, you are graced,
The phenomenal human.

STORM

Storm, storm, strong storm
Storm in many shades and forms
Storm of life, storm of sea
With wavelengths and frequencies
High pitch and rigid current
Plain strength and raw will
Storming everything, everywhere.

Storm, storm, pushing up
Storm, storm, pushing down
Marching out wonderful order
Ticking, ticking, always,
Colour party, marching out.

Phenomenal storm, in life
Known, unknown, natural, manmade
Captivating, devastating
O choose to be captivating.

Be that phenomenal storm
Destroy foundations of lust
Crush platforms of greed
Let envy and selfishness die,
Be that phenomenon
Let the world be free.

HATE

Hate, ungodly hate
Roaring here and there
Killing lives anyhow.

Hate, hate, barbaric
Wasting lives speedily
Rolling, none stop.

Hate, O hate this hate
Hate all that is ungodly
Fight hate in totality
Cast it out from mankind.

Be the phenomenal fighter
Win it in generality
Kill it in all sense
Let it be your duty.

Phenomenal hate against evil
Stamp it out off the living
Crash it, scrap it, loose it
Let the world be phenomenally free from hate.

DREAM

Dream big, dream large
Not just when you sleep
Dream great, dream real
Not just when you snur.

Dream, please dream well
See vision and revelations
Dream, please dream again
See future and answers
Let us recreate this world
And make it more phenomenal.

Dream, alas, dream
Let nobody steal your dream
Dream, dream, keep dreaming
Let no situation capture you
Dream aloud, dream anew
Forget yesterday, your sorrow
See tomorrow, see the unborn
Please keep dreaming.

You are a phenomenal dream
Yes, you can make it
Push, pray, work it, it is possible.

SLEEP

We need sleep by nature
We sleep to ease off
And regain energy
Sleep is a refill
It renews strength and refreshes.

Humans sleep, living things do
Humans rest especially during sleep
Sleeping revitalizes the body.

It is necessary to sleep
Sleeping is a therapy too,
We wake up with newness,
Fresh thoughts, mind and soul
Ready for next work
But sleep not away time.

Sleeping can be harmful
Sleeping sickness does no good
Put your fears to sleep
And wake up the giant in you
You are a hero, a lion
Roar, soar, lead aright
Be a phenomenal human.

THIRST

It is a lack, a want
An urge longing to be satisfied,
A yearning to be met.

Thirst is raw and natural
It does not segregate
It is a cell of nature
No living thing escapes it.

Thirst is mandatory
The Creator made it so
We satisfy it when it calls
We obey whenever we answer.

Thirst is a force, a pull
A push against self
A desire to be met,
Be thirsty, long for good
Desire to satisfy thirst
People's thirst, the world's thirst
Thirst for phenomenal things.

HUNGER

Hunger, an emptiness
A wandering, to settle
A wondering to understand
Hunger is as old as creation.

Hunger brought creation
Hunger caused discovery
Hunger exhumed multiplication
Hunger is beyond magic.

Magical hunger, hunger for peace
Monumental hunger, hunger for unity
Hunger for life, hunger for love
Hunger to be accepted.

Hunger is natural, it is a craving
When treated, one knows calm
But when not, there is trouble.

Hunger for good, hunger for freedom
Hunger for greatness and liberty
Do not hunger for bread
Bread does not satisfy the world
Nor the soul,
Reach out for phenomenal hunger.

Ngozi Olivia Osuoha

LOVE

Love is a universal language
It has a unique voice
And it speaks volume.

Love is a forceful pull
 It is magnetic and deep,
It travels across boundaries.

Love is a god on its own
It transcends human compression
Comprehension dares it not,
Love is light yet the weightiest,
It flies, it runs, it swims.

Love is a propagation
It does not dwell on propaganda
Love is a mirror
It reflects oneself accurately.

Love is a phenomenon
It does phenomenal wonders,
Only phenomenal humans capture it
Be phenomenal, love real and deep
Love encompasses other phenomena.

WILL

Will is a strong force
It wills as it pleases
Will is a wheel
It wheels as it wills.

Will is a cycle, a point
It rotates, revolves, resounds
It resolves, reminiscences, rewinds
Love is resilient, like the will
Will is a love, a true love.

Will is critical, and analytical
It possess raw strength
And drives long for so long.

Will is complex, and compound
Its interest is firm and rigid
Will supports intentions, especially good.

Will is phenomenal, be a will
Will the wheel of your will
Will it to your wheel, fix it willfully
Be a phenomenon, be human
A phenomenal human follows his will.

Ngozi Olivia Osuoha

PASSION

Passion is a crazy force
It propels and compels
Passion is charming
It motivates and inspires.

Passion is green
Always alive, no matter when
Passion is rainbow
Always beautiful, no matter what.

Passion is loud
Bold and outstanding
Passion is straight
Even alone and lonely.

Passion stands firm
Speaking in one voice
Never contradictory
Passion knows her mind,
And she follows through.

Passionate people fail too,
But they never quit
Passion is phenomenal
It does phenomenal things
Route for phenomenal passion.

DANCE

Dance mature
The body moves according to sound
Sometimes, there may be no sound
Yet the body dances
Expressing the melody of the soul.

Music is the rhythm of life
Life is the rhythm of self,
Music heals, music entertains
Dance and dancing are awesome.

Dance is a time
Not just of musical instruments
Dance is a performance
It can be poor or rich
It can be woeful or beautiful.

Dance is a nuance of the soul
A wonderful expression of the spirit,
It bears the burden of ease.

Dance, dance to phenomena
Give a phenomenal rendition
Get applauded, rounds of applause
Let the stage feel your phenomenal dance.

Ngozi Olivia Osuoha

HUMANITY

Humanity is the crux
Nothing exists outside it.

Humanity is the foundation
Everything is built on it,
Humanity is the pivot
It suspends all others
Humanity is the rock
It supports the world.

Let it grow and flourish
Let it rise and tower up
Let humanity spread its wings
For in flying we take solace.

You are humanity, the only true one
Focus on salvage and rescue
For humanity is fast slipping away.

Be that phenomenal human
For humanity is phenomenal too.

Bear the torch of humanity
Shine it in all dark places
Let the phenomenal light shine on.

AGE

Age, is age forever
Nothing changes that fact
Age is yesterday, today and tomorrow.

Age was, is, and will be
Age has been, it is always
Phenomenal age, time ancient and modern.

Age buries events and chances
In it are opportunities and lucks
Be on the queue, align to it
The phenomenal age has humans.

Age with grace and grease
Grace all ages phenomenally
Dead or alive, stand out
Because you are a phenomenal human.

Age tells stories and histories
Age whispers on the ears,
Age salutes courage
Age recounts endeavours
Yes, age too mourns the lost
You had better been phenomenal.

Ngozi Olivia Osuoha

PUZZLE

Life is a puzzle
It bewilders the great
And confuses the wise,
Life is a puzzle
It weakens the strong
And strengthens the weak,
Life is a puzzle
It complicates simplicity
And simplifies complexity.

Life is a puzzle
It builds several ceilings
And shatters many more.

Life is a deep puzzle
Sophisticated and raw,
Be a living soul
Solve this puzzle,
Be a puzzle, a puzzle-solver
Yes, because you are a phenomenal human.

Puzzles require deep thinking
Concentration, focus and creativity
Creativeness, and abilities
Be one, have them all
Remain phenomenal.

QUESTION

Life is a question itself
It is full of questions
Questions that plead for answers
And answers that are far.

Questions dry reasons
Reasons of less answers
Answers of weightless values
Values that elode sanity.

Life is crazy
It requires craziness
At least sometimes,
According to discernment.

Be a question to the world
Wonder the world to the last
Let questions answer you.

Remain a question, solve many
The world boils questions
Phenomenal answers they need
Surprise them, let them keep asking
The phenomenal human will answer them
And that is you.

FUTURE

Future is unknown
It is more mysterious than the past,
It glows and dims
Looking great and brick too.

Future is a puzzle
A phenomenal puzzle,
It creates doubts and ripples
High frequency, low trace
Reverberation of faint echoes
Future is a long journey.

Future is an imagination
It is a dream, a reflection
Sometimes, a mirage
No one holds it firm.

Future is slippery as well
It can track anyone down
It can trace anybody up,
Future raises chances
And makes phenomenal histories.

Be the future, the future of the world
You lead phenomenal ideas
And brand foundations
Be future, be futuristic.

HISTORY

History is of the world
It keeps records for tomorrow
And builds plaque for posterity.

History is of men
They decide how it will be
Positive or negative,
We create history in our time.

Be historical, be a history
Write it bold and clear
Upon bricks, stones and marbles.

Make historical; phenomena
Paste it on walls of the world
Let the living read it
Let the unborn also do,
For the dead would be seeing it.

The phenomenal human is you
Lead through this valley
Let the spectrum of light shine
Glow fantastically for life.

LEGACY

Except one leaves one or more,
One has not lived
Except one bears fruit
One has not really lived.

Legacy is of uncountable types
We live according to destiny
Legacies are left by humans
Phenomenal humans leave phenomenal legacies.

Legacies of life and time
Legacies of events and occasions,
Legacies of colours and wonders.

Legends are big and small
Poor and rich, black and white,
They come from anywhere
They go through a lot in life
They are humans like others.

Leave phenomenal legacies
Be a phenomenal legend
Make yourself a legacy,
For the phenomenal human does wonders.

THEORY

Theory of theorems
Theorems of equations
Equations of life,
Life of balanced and imbalanced principles.

The theory of life
One which catapults causes
And protracts courses
Restraining curses and effects,
Even after being catalysts.

The theory of life
Propagations of illumination
Illumination of radiations,
Radiations of ultraviolet rays.

Rays of life, beaming rays
Phenomenal rays of human
Capturing phenomena.

Yes, theories of mesmerizing questions
Supporting beams and columns
Columns of inordinate objects
Objecting reasons and answers
Projecting answers from phenomenal men.

Ngozi Olivia Osuoha

ADVENTURE

You are an adventure
Let the world explore you.

You are an adventure
Let the world discover you.

You then learn and relearn
Let them unlearn, bridle and unbridle.

Yes, you too are an adventurer
Learn from them, explore them
Learn from the world.

Never let go of any chance
Utilize every opportunity
Hang in, in that voyage of discovery
Lead, as you follow the compass.

Sail, swim and row
This ship may not anchor
The sea may be very dry
The sky may not be cloudy
The land may be swampy
Only phenomenal humans can cope.

Adjust, readjustment is necessary
Focus, focus is important
Learn to be dynamic
But in all things, never forget your mission.

INNOVATION

Innovation is done by men
Men, extraordinary.

Innovation is done by humans
Humans, phenomenal.

Innovation is a challenge,
Accept it even from daredevils.

Innovation is a tug-of-war
Throw all your weight behind it.

Innovation is a performing stage
Right there, win it loud.

Phenomenal innovations
Innovations by phenomenal humans,
Write the story, the history
Let your name bear it
Let it bear your name,
Your phenomenal name.

JUSTICE

Justice, the bane
Justice, the rose of love
Justice, the voice of freedom.

Give it, demand it
Far or near, never be quiet
Lest it dies off the world.

Justice is a cap of purity
It signifies peace and equity
Justice is a coat of unity
It calms trouble and fight.

Justice prolongs life
It serves humanity too,
It is a clean melody
That resonates in serenity.

You are therefore a phenomenal justice
Let not the arm be cut off
Lest generations unborn suffer
Live it, earn it, embrace it
Shout it, spread it, birth it, pamper it
Justice is everything.

UNITY

Unity is an umbrella
It shelters heads
Unity is a tree
It has many branches.

An umbrella of love
A tree of one accord
An umbrella of serenity
A tree of thousands of fruits.

Unity is a song
It talks of sounds
Sounds of peace
Sounds of oneness,
Those of progress and gratitude
Unity is a fertile Iroko.

Cultivate it, water it
Prune and weed it
Fertilize it, harvest it
Store it for the future,
Make it phenomenal
Because it is mighty and necessary.

PEACE

Peace is a child
Do not make him an orphan
Peace is a youth
Do not make him wayward
Peace is a woman
Do not make her a widow.

Peace is a father
Do not make him promiscuous
Peace is an uncle
Do not make him jealous
Peace is a relative
Do not keep him afar.

Peace is phenomenal
It is the bedrock of growth
Peace is a mirror
It is the reflection of the society,
Peace is a voice
It is the echo of the living
Glue to peace, take a clue from the rest
Phenomenal humans love peace
Because they fight no wars.

EQUITY

Equity tells of justice
It speaks of equality
It portrays one voice.

Equity asks for cleanness
It does not cheat
It stands out loud
And poses outstandingly.

Equity is a phenomenon
It wages wars automatically
Equity answers natural laws
It speaks sheets for comfort.

They love it, they question it
They accept it, they reject it
They do, they say, they stop
But equity is at peace.

Phenomenon of equity, great
Phenomenal humans, adjusting
Lifting up one voice in support
Rolling out drums of passion.

Ngozi Olivia Osuoha

SIGN

You are a sign and a wonder
You are a wonder and a sign
Sign it with a wonder
Let them wonder the sign.

Signs are for great people
They live it above humans,
They bow, they stoop, they win
The signs glitter from above.

Signs and wonders dazzle
Neither perishable nor tangible
They shine beyond reach
And startle the ordinary.

Ordinary people wonder far
They are astonished and amazed
Because they cannot comprehend;
Phenomenal humans glow more and more.

The sign is very phenomenal
Because humans ponder on puzzles
As phenomenal humans grow deep and deeper
Gathering momentum and velocity
Accelerating speedily,
Reaching phenomenal heights.

MISSION

Living is a mission
Mission is a living
Living through the mission
Mission through the living,
One can find the connection.

Mission is a gift
It has to be useful
Mission is a life
Live it, maintain its lifespan.

Live your mission
And mission your life
The purpose, the mission, the goal
Only you can do.

Phenomenal missions of voices
Voicing the missions aloud
Even in a coarse and harsh world.

Mission accomplished, right or wrong
Phenomenal humans, right
Chase it, lift it, offer it all
You are that phenomenal soul.

ECLIPSE

Eclipse of the sun
Eclipse of the moon
Eclipse of the earth
Eclipse around the globe.

Nature, responding to call
Aligning, retreating, surrendering
Moving up and down
Taking shapes and forms
Trying to suit themselves,
At a particular time.

Eclipse of tides
Eclipse of times
Eclipse of waves
Eclipse of storms
Tempest, turbulence
Troubles in and out
Fights, all around
All, eclipse of some kind.

Eclipse in the world
Eclipse in the sea
Eclipse in the air,
Eclipse of nature
Eclipse of the universe
Wonders and wonderment.

Be an eclipse, at least once
Yes, be that phenomenal
Human, in the form of an eclipse
Eclipsing human as a phenomenon.

Block evil, release good
Grow kindness, object wickedness
Let darkness be gone.

POPULATION

Population is a wonder
It grows, it reduces, it fluctuates
Up and down, sideways
It just moves any direction.

Population is useful
Especially when big,
It can also be a nuisance
Especially when growing in crime.
Population records numbers
Birth, death, stillbirth, disabled
Mostly, when dealing with humans.

Population is a phenomenon
Phenomenal humans make it up,
You had better been one.

Do not just be a number
And never just be a member,
Be unique, be spectacular, be countable.

Use the population effectively
Let everyone count
Stand up and be counted.

CLIMATE

Climate of the world
Affecting nooks and crannies
Dealing with humans
Telling all over the world.

Climate of the universe
Disturbing, still disturbing
Changing, saturating, changing and over-saturating
Causing harm and oppositions
Forcing talks and activism.

Climate of stormy days
Climate of troubled earth
Climate of restless world
Climate of warring universe,
Tearing hopes and calm lands
Washing off, waters of peaceful thirst.

Be phenomenal climate
Fight this ugly change back
Let your labour be phenomenal.

Be a climate
A good one
Let the climate around you be great
Move with peacefulness,
Be a mild climate
The one we need.

TEMPERATURE

Temperature is a degree
The degree of hotness or coldness
Especially of a body.

Be hot, when needed
Be cold, when necessary
Be warm at worst.

Temperature is a phenomenon
It tells of bodies,
Be a thermometer, read bodies
Read better, yet be a temperature.

Temperature is important
Our abodes say of them
Temperature is unique
The world never minds.

Read yours, know yours
Know where you belong
Be a phenomenal body-reader
Not just about the physical.

Ngozi Olivia Osuoha

NATURAL DISASTERS

War is a natural disaster
Though caused by man,
Tornadoes ruin humans
And wreck properties,
Landslides do horrors
And barely spare,
Earthquakes quake in magnitudes
Breaking even altitudes,
Natural disasters devour like wolves
They are just horrific.

Forces of untold powers
Climbing and clamping down on man
Tearing the world apart
Fighting to leave ruins
Ruins and heaps of ruins.

Phenomenal disasters, natural
Unimaginable harm and destruction
Look, see, that you destroy not
Build the world with your might
For the world is half gone already.

Do phenomenal changes, render help
Show mercy, show love
Natural disasters have done enough.

ACT OF GOD

When certain things happen, we watch
We get more confused
We seek answers, even wrongly.

When things happen, we wonder
We attribute them to so many things,
But there is one, so special;
The act of God.

Good or bad, known or unknown
Seen or unseen, great or small
These acts of God, glitter
They are always conspicuous.

In life, in death, home or abroad
Far or near, within or without
These acts speak volumes,
They sound loud like thunder
And refect like lightning.

They are phenomenal
They perform wonder
Be the act of God
Let those who see you believe.

Ngozi Olivia Osuoha

RACISM

Racism, a manmade act
Act of cowardice and ignorance
By people who do not understand,
Who are poor to face reality,
The reality that the world is vast
And does not revolve around them.

Racism, a hateful act by monsters
By those who seek to devour others
Who use and abuse others,
Who still question God for His creativity.

Racism, a tripod of hate, bigotry and greed
A pot of selfishness
Racism, a beast of lust
The bed of fear, complex and dominance.

Say no to racism, stop it
Bury it, burn it down
Let it die, live and let live.

Accept others made by the Maker
Skin colour, hair colour, eyes
Body, voice, accent, tone, differ
And their culture, religion, belief, not yours.

Stop the violence, let love lead
Give peace a chance
Be a phenomenal human
Live a phenomenal life,
Kick out racism, totally.

GERMINATION

Germination is a mystery, a puzzle
It baffles beyond explanation
The wonder behind it
The patience, process and chemistry
The logic, rational and irrational
All, make germination a compounded issue.

Only seeds germinate
And they do not, except they die,
They bury their flesh and body
And then rise to a new life.

You are a seed
For you to germinate
You must die, die to the flesh
Bury your pride and shame
Forfeit your comfort zone
Dig deep, and exhume raw gold.

Germinate therefore, you are a phenomenal seed
Shatter the limits and barriers
Break the soil and rise
Destroy anything holding you back
Fight off the boundary
Dismantle the roadblocks
Scatter the cage
For your growth is anticipated.

Grow, shine, break forth
Come, glow, in full force
You are a phenomenal human
Phenomenal things await your reign.

BREATH

Breathing is the evidence that you are alive
Breathing supplies air, to sustain life
And gives hope.

Breathing is a wonder
The air, and it's commonness
The breath and its uncommonness,
We breathe, we live
We die, if we cease breathing
The breath of life is deep.
It searches far beyond answers
The breath of life satisfies
Yes, it supports existence
And cares for living.

Be the breath, not just to breathe
Purify breath, simplify them
Give people breath, and let them live
For breathing ceases in a twinkle.

Breathing is phenomenal,
We breathe phenomenon
And phenomenally,
Once gone, forever lost
Forever lost, there it ends.

THUNDER

Thunder is an act of God
It is a heavenly body
It goes with lightning too.
With loud sound, high pitch
Sometimes, little but noticeable,
Heard, acknowledged and talked of
Thunders are never shy.

Thunders cultivate a lot
They plant too,
Fear, shock, courage, boldness, bravery
Thunders untie what they wish.

Strong powers of self-will
Harbouring delicate issues
Hurt, hurting lines of unconsciousness
Thwarting wants and needs.

Thunders travel clear, direct or indirect
They choose their paths
They see no obstruction
Despite what we see.

Be a thunder, bear your lightning
Create sounds, sounds of amazing frequency
Make them foolish for fooling you
Whoever tries to stop the phenomena,
Let them realize you are a phenomenon.

Ngozi Olivia Osuoha

RELATIONSHIPS

The world is a relationship
Everything in it is a relationship too.
The world dwells in relationships
And fosters numerous relationships,
The world is a relation.

Relationships between humans, animals
Nations, continents, even planets
And the worlds beyond,
The world is a manager
A relationship manager,
Managing the affairs of living and non living things.
Be a phenomenal manager
Manage relations, relationships, relatives
Non relatives, friends, and others,
Let them know you exist or once existed.

Relationships grow sour or bitter sometimes
Make and break, break and quench
Human, manmade, and natural factors
Relationships can be smooth
They can be productive, or anything,
Facilitate the sides of relations
Cause phenomenal effects.

Phenomenal humans leave phenomenal traces
They make their footprints bold
So that relationships thrive on them,
Be a phenomenal relative and friend
It pays to sit well.
Traces, footpaths and footsteps
Theses tell who we are, who we were
And what we would or would have been,
Carefully plant yours.

NATURAL RESOURCES

Raw, great and rich
They come in diverse forms
Colours, in different shades
Sizes, in many stars
For different needs and plans.

Natural resources from nature
Some need a little touch
Some undergo refining
Some extraction, examination
They yield revenues and incomes.

For trades, local and foreign
For consumption, within and without
For exchange, beyond borders
For relationship of many calibres
Local, national, international
Natural resources bring interactions.

For unions, orders, fraternities, friendships
For income, exposure, discoveries
Natural resources are phenomenal,
You are part of the natural resources too.

Be refined locally, nationally, internationally
Do phenomenal things like natural resources
Be better than pure gold, diamond and oil.

VEGETATION

Green and lively, large and great
Flourishing beyond greatness and greenness
Overflowing in production, regeneration
Feeding nations in many ways.

Yes, phenomenal, it is
All vegetations, no matter what
Times and forces fight them
Times and forces defend them too,
Be time, be force.

You too are a vegetation
Vegetation in human form
Grow, plant, weed, prune
Learn, change, develop, exercise
Discover, recover, broaden your scope
Be phenomenal, humanity is deep
The human is deeper.

Vegetations are green, but not all
However, they colour, they grow
They break boundaries always
Irrespective of attacks, known or unknown
Let your vegetation never die
You are unique, a special specie,
Out of the world's numerous vegetations.

MARRIAGE

Marriage is a wonderful union
It brings people together
People of opposite sex
They learn to live together.

People from different backgrounds
With different beliefs and visions
Diverse experiences and careers
Sometimes different race and religions
They accept to be together in marriage.

Marriage is phenomenal
It has been from the ages
And it will remain through ages
Despite the turbulence it faces.

Marriage produces children
Children of many callings and passions.

Marriage seals relationships
And creates new and numerous ones
Marriage is a great mystery.

It is not always smooth
And so is life, up and down
Nothing is perfect, not humans.

Marry yourself first, your mission
Blend it with your passion
And your partner,
Arrive at a better place
Strive not to fall because of marriage,
Rather let it lift you
Be a phenomenal spouse.

DIVORCE

Divorce comes after marriage
That is, as a result of bad marriage
People hardly divorce from good marriage
In fact, many remain in bad marriage.

Divorce is a phenomenon
And it has saved some lives,
No matter what.

Some societies view it as a taboo
Some see it as spiritual problem
Some love it, some embrace it happily
While some pray for it.

Many people have died out of bad marriage
Especially women, who could not walk away
Divorce has also scattered some dreams
Especially children from divorced partners.

It is better to stay alive comfortably as a divorcee
Than remain in an abusive marriage
The bondage of marrying a wrong spouse
The pain of losing concentration,
The agony of separating unwillingly
The burden of disappointment
The shame of being stigmatized
All, and more do more harm.

Stigmas attached to divorce in some places
In some timid and crude societies,
In places frustrated by religion
In lands brainwashed with culture,
These places do more horrors,
Especially to women and children.

Divorce is a phenomenon
No right thinking person really wants it
But it saves life, sometimes properties.

Some marry rich people, to dump them
They fly divorce and file it
Maybe after some children
And use that as a pipeline,
To syphon money from them.

Ngozi Olivia Osuoha

MOUNTAIN

Phenomenal nature, high or not
Wonderful and amazing
Crazy to behold
In lands far and wide.

Mountain of great heights
Towering up to the sky
Attracting tourists and mountaineers
Yielding revenues too.

Mountains are phenomenal
They serve as boundaries
They also serve as defences,
Especially in times of war.

Mountains create adventures
They give pleasures and happiness,
Especially to those that love them.

Explorers visit them
Researchers do, too
Tourists tour them
Climbers climb as well,
Mountains are phenomena.

It takes strength to climb them
Encouragement, courage and bravery
It takes determination to face it
Decision, choice and legendary.

Be a mountain, let the strong climb
Be a mountain, attract explorers and tourists
Let researchers come, and climbers
Be the guide, the guard, the mountaineer
Be brave, be courageous, be bold
Be phenomenal, the phenomenal human.

LEARNING

Man is born to learn
From the womb, he starts learning
Growing, adjusting and readjusting
In order to live in this world.

Born, he starts being breastfed
Suckling, the breast is learning, too
From days, to weeks, to months, to years
He keeps learning and growing
In order to be a man.

Teething, crawling, standing, staggering, walking, talking
All and many more are processes of learning.

At home, bathing, washing, cleaning, cooking
House chores and timing,
He starts becoming the man.

At school, later, different subjects
At home, respect, discipline, do's and dont's
In the society, he learns left and right
Cultures, traditions, norms and values
Religion, he learns beliefs, disbeliefs, and others.

All the groups, agents of change
All the agents of socialization
All, formal and informal

With personal wisdom, thinking, ability, gifts
Coupled with the purpose in life
Mission, vision, destiny, talent,
He learns, relearns, unlearns, and the cycle continues.

That way, he becomes a better person
Because learning is a phenomenon,
A continuous process, till death
A steady process, world without end.

Ngozi Olivia Osuoha

GALAXY

A group of stars, up there
Shining unto the earth
Tickling the sky
Mesmerizing the world.

A group of stars
A cluster, twinkling
Sparkling in awe,
Illuminating nature against darkness.

Galaxy, galaxies, cluster of stars
Chasing away darkness and gloom
Sending them to hell
In the innermost part.

Be a galaxy, that galaxy
The phenomenal galaxy that shines
The shine that gives hope
The hope that brightens nights.

Yes, you are, you can be
Be the galaxy, a bunch of stars
In groups, clusters, and fragments
This light and shine dare not die.

VOICE

The voice of the people
The voice of the poor
The downtrodden and the forgotten
The abused and the misused
The violated and the exploited
Be their voice, phenomenal voice.

Yes, you are a voice
Be their voice, speak
Keep speaking
Let the world hear you.

Speak up for them
Speak out against evil
Help the needy, the poor
The voiceless and the intimidated,
Voice out for them.

Your voice is phenomenal
You are the phenomenal human,
Help them, hear them, save them.

Hear them too, hear their voice
Listen deep, listen long, listen patiently
They are talking, they are speaking
They wail and cry, they weep and mourn
Please hear them too,
The phenomenal listener.

Ngozi Olivia Osuoha

BLOOD

Blood is a phenomenon
Though mammals have it,
It is red in all
We bleed same.

Blood is strong, no matter whose
Shedding it digs a pit
A pit of numerous falls.

Blood is amazing
It sustains humans, mammals
No man survives without blood.

Be like blood, help others survive
Live in others, flow in them
Support their living, stop their dying
Let nothing lead you to killing them.

Blood is sacred, it is holy
People joke with it, people sacrifice it,
 Unfortunately at ungodly altars
Desist from Bloodshedding.

Be phenomenal blood
Give it, save it, retain it, maintain it, sustain it
Blood also means relatives, relationships
Keep them sacred, keep them safe.

ORIGIN

Origin is natural from birth
It cannot be thwarted
Though we try.

Origin is Godgiven
It is not actually chosen
Origin is beyond man
No matter how he manipulates.

Be your origin, be original
Defend it, safeguard it
Nothing is more precious
Your origin is a phenomenon,
Use it for phenomenal purposes.

Ngozi Olivia Osuoha

RACE

No matter our skin colour
We are where we come from,
Our race is inborn
Normal and natural
We dare not switch it.

Processes and methods emerge
Styles of, and for being from another race
But race is race, it is solely natural.

Born into any race, mixed or one
Yes, you are there
Marriage, naturalization, oaths
They only change the physical, and temporal.

Phenomenal is the race
Our race is constant actually
And none is superior nor inferior,
Accept it, deal with it, it is that way
Use it too, for phenomenal purposes.

PARENT

Parents are many
In diverse forms and lands
Paternal, maternal, social, spiritual,
Political, financial, educational, and others
They all do wonders in our lives.

Natural parents remain the truest
Foster, adopted, adoptive, master, lords, surrogate
They all have boundaries.

But natural parents are phenomenal
Nothing changes that,
Hate, love, poverty, separation, divorce,
Abuse, war, death, disownment,
Nothing, whatsoever changes that phenomenal fact.

Be a parent, like a natural parent
Father, mother children for the world
Parents love real, they love hard
They sacrifice, all forms of sacrifice
You can, you too can, because you are a phenomenon.

CHANGE

Change is a great mystery
It goes on with or without us,
It may not require our consent.

Change is natural
It pierces every wall
And cracks limits,
Change faults ceilings
And bruises barriers.

Change advances
Yes, it does, left or right
Up or down
It takes extraordinary power to stop change,
If you ever dare, depending on its route.

Be change, positive change
Be changeful with speed, though slow
Be like a wildfire, light up the world
Be that phenomenal change
The world seeks you, yes.

FIGHT

There are various types of fight in life
We fight all through our lifetime
We fight with factors and rates
We fight with forces, seen and unseen
We fight knowingly and unknowingly,
Everything is a fight.

From the rising of the sun to its setting
From birth to death
All the stages of life
Fights go on, within and without.

Daily, we fight
We struggle with life, in life, for life
We plough and till, both on land and on high.

Face the fight, fight it phenomenally
Win loud, clear and crystal
You are a phenomenal human, remember.

SIBLINGS

There are times we err, as humans
There are times we lose it
When we cannot comprehend why and how,
No matter what we do or become,
It never wipes out the phenomenon of sibling-hood.

Siblings remain siblings, forever
Dead, alive, disowned, separated
Abandoned, rejected, mad, sick
Quarreled, announced, hidden
The fact remains, same blood runs and flows.

Same parents or parent had them
They are irreversible, no matter what
Sibling-hood is a phenomenon
We cannot shave it off,
Deal with it, love your siblings
Support them, tomorrow is a mystery.

FOUNDER

Founders are phenomenal
They are pure genius
With or without formal education.

Founders hold on for long
They pass through tests and trials
They fail sometimes, they move on still.

Some died at the cost
Some lost for the course,
Some, bullied for the cross,
Yet, they held on.

Some were even dumped by colleagues
Partners in the same boat
Forerunners and pathfinders
Some gave in their best wrongly.

Be a founder, a phenomenal foundation
Find things the world needs
Things to propel the world,
Things that would ease tension,
Phenomenal discoveries and inventions
Because you are a phenomenon.

Ngozi Olivia Osuoha

CREATIVITY

You are creativity, the bunch
In you, are the root and stem
The branches grow from you
And fruits bear greatly.

You are creativity, yes, you
Creativity is a phenomenon
It is awesome, and wonderful
Creative people go places
Create, procreate, recreate.

Creativity saves a lot
It teaches a bunch too
Be creative and inspirational
Inspire the world, rule,
Build a world of phenomenal creativity.

Phenomenal creativity beckons
Hear it calling your name
Answer, and save the world
Yes, you alone can do great things
Because you are a phenomenal human.

FRUITS

You are a fruit
Fruit of a marvelous seed
Be sweet, be kind, be generous.

Fruits heal and save lives
Fruits supplement and augment,
Fruits generate incomes and revenues
Be fruitful, bear fruits.

Fruits bring transportation
It causes foreign exchange
Yes, it opens borders.

Ripe on time do not decay
Taste great and serve flavours
Let those who taste you live
For phenomenal fruits produce life,
They bear fruits of purity,
Because they are from seeds of excellent services.

SKILL

Learn a trade, get a skill
Trades fix homes, skills connect the world.

Trade your fear, skill your skill
Trade your doubts, skin your skill
Trades and skills are helpful.

Yes, you are a trade, a stock in trade
You are a skill, a skillful skeleton,
You will never die, you live forever
Be great, be ready, be prepared
Go vast, learn versatility.

Skills answer so many calls
Trades sponsor diverse missions
Explore and exploit their scopes,
You are a phenomenon, so they are
Reach out, find them, find us, find the world.

FLEXIBILITY

Man is flexible, yes he is
Because life is not static
Changes happen daily,
So does man trying to fit in.

Flexibility is a phenomenon
Be flexible, be phenomenal
It saves traumas and troubles.

Back and forth, like a pendulum
Up and down, like a ball
Left and right, like hands of time
Learn flexibility, support it
Because rigidity is timid and awkward.

Ngozi Olivia Osuoha

AGILITY

Flesh and bone are a couple
They dance and twist
Out of joints, within joints
They stay, they shift, they dislocate
They bond, they tear, they fracture.

Agility is part of life
The human body knows it well
Agility is a phenomenon
Some humans are very agile
Some are stiff, dull, and slow,
Be agile, be flexible, be vigilant, be gallant.

Agility is a link, a line, it connects
Bones flow, they dance, they bend
They take forms according to situations.

Agility is necessary
It helps at some points,
The phenomenal human is agile.

REPRODUCTION

Reproduction is a phenomenon
No matter how prevalent it is
It is the flow of life
The baton of relay in life,
From generation to generation.

Reproduction is a phenomenon
Phenomenal humans reproduce,
Animals do, too.

Reproduction is very important
It paves ways for growth
It stabilizes kinds and species,
Especially the human race
And propels lineages.

Reproduction is an act of God
An ordinance made by Him
A decree and order,
Phenomenally given to phenomenal humans.

There are times reproduction is hard
There are humans who may not
Due to sickness, disease or choice,
It does not make them less human,
Because humans are phenomenal breeds.

LUST

Lust is a phenomenon too
Despite the negative effects
Lust causes damages and dangers
It does more harm than good.

Lustful people can rape, kill
They can dupe, steal, lie and elope
Lust is a trademark of ill
It does not really end well.

Lust is tight, it can be anyone
It is harmful and deadly
It does not spare religion or faith,
It cuts across tongues, tribes and race,
It never builds a home, not a good one.

Do not be lustful
Be a phenomenal human of positivity
Change the circumstances to good and for good
Let it end in praise and honour.

URGE

Urge is a normal thing
It rides in men
It creates the fire to do anything.

Urge is a passion
Wasteful or useful,
It is the zeal that runs
The heat and hotness that burn,
That sudden overwhelming and overtaking
It could be in any direction.

It runs back and forth
It can choose any method
But meant to be controlled
Self discipline pays
Self esteem and self worth help
They put the control checks and stoppers.

Urge is of many types
Positive urges do positive things
Negative urges do negative things
Have positive urge, do positive things
Give pleasures, happiness and great vibes,
Be an urge, phenomenal urge
Let the world celebrate your urges.

Ngozi Olivia Osuoha

THE PHENOMENAL HUMAN

The phenomenal human is outstanding
He is not as ordinary as he appears
The phenomenal human is a light
He is a lamp in the dark.

He is a voice in the wildernesses
He is an oasis in the desert
He is the rose among thorns
He speaks, he flourishes, he survives.

Though his journey is not always smooth
But his destination is always sure,
He is an accomplisher
He rules his world kingly
And loves his life, no matter what.

The phenomenal human is fully human
But he is on a destined journey,
Serpents, scorpions, adders and thorns
Horrors, fears, darkness and hunger
All, and many more dare not stop him,
In fact, they get tired of trying him.

Ngozi Olivia Osuoha

The Phenomenal Human

Ngozi Olivia Osuoha is a Nigerian poet, writer and thinker. A graduate of Estate Management with experience in Banking and Broadcasting.

She has eighteen poetry books published in Kenya, Canada, the Philippines, USA, and others. She has also co-authored one (with Kenyan literary critic Amos O. Ojwang').

She has been featured in over sixty-five international anthologies and also has published over two hundred and fifty poems and articles in over twenty countries.

Many of her poems have been translated and published into other languages, including Spanish, Russian, Romanian, Polish, Khloe, Farsi, and Arabic, among others.

She has won many awards; she is a one time *Best of the Net* nominee, and she has numerous words on marble.

www.ingramcontent.com/pod-product-compliance
Lightning Source LLC
Chambersburg PA
CBHW030057100526
44591CB00008B/189